D1567197

Martial Arts for
Special Forces

MARTIAL AND FIGHTING ARTS SERIES

Judo

Jujutsu

Karate

Kickboxing

Kung Fu

Martial Arts for Athletic Conditioning

Martial Arts for Children

Martial Arts for the Mind

Martial Arts for People with Disabilities

Martial Arts for Special Forces

Martial Arts for Women

Ninjutsu

Taekwondo

Martial Arts for Special Forces

CHRIS McNAB

Senior Consultant Editor
Aidan Trimble (6th Dan)
Former World, European, and
British Karate Champion
Chairman and Chief Instructor to the
Federation of Shotokan Karate

MASON CREST PUBLISHERS
www.masoncrest.com

Mason Crest Publishers Inc.
370 Reed Road
Broomall, PA, 19008
(866) MCP-BOOK (toll free)
www.masoncrest.com

2 3 4 5 6 7 8 9 10

McNab, Chris.
Martial arts for the special forces / Chris McNab.
v. cm. -- (Martial and fighting arts)
Includes bibliographical references (p.) and index.
Contents: What are special forces? -- Military unarmed combat --
Training to fight -- Attacking the enemy -- Defensive tactics --
Grappling and special techniques -- Glossary -- Further reading --
Special Forces of the world.

ISBN 1-59084-400-9 (hardcover)
1. Hand-to-hand fighting--Juvenile literature. 2. Special forces
(Military science)--Juvenile literature. [1. Hand-to-hand fighting. 2.
Martial arts. 3. Special forces (Military science)] I. Title. II. Series.
GV1111.M39 2003
355.5'48--dc21
2002155769

Editorial and design by
Amber Books Ltd.
Bardley's Close
74-77 White Lion Street
London N1 9PF
www.amberbooks.co.uk

Project Editor Chris Stone
Design www.stylus-design.com
Picture Research Lisa Wren

Color reproduction by MRM Graphics, England
Printed and bound in the Hashemite Kingdom of Jordan.

IMPORTANT NOTICE
The techniques and information described in this publication are for use in dire circumstances only where
the safety of the individual is at risk. Accordingly, the publisher cannot accept any responsibility for any
prosecution or proceedings brought or instituted against any person or body as a result of the use or misuse
of the techniques and information within.

Contents

Introduction

When I began studying the martial arts back in 1972, the whole subject was shrouded in mystery; indeed, that was part of the attraction. At that time there was only a limited range of books on the subject and therefore very little information was available to the novice.

I am glad to say that this has changed in recent years beyond all recognition. With the explosion of interest in the martial arts and the vast array of quality books that are now on the market, we seem to be increasing our knowledge and understanding of the martial arts and sports science, and this fact is reflected in this new series of books.

Over the past 30 years, I have been privileged to compete, train, and teach with practitioners from most of the disciplines covered in this series. I have coached world champions, developed and adapted training methods for people with disabilities, and instructed members of the armed forces in close-quarter techniques. I can warmly recommend this series as a rich source of information for students and instructors alike. Books can never replace a good instructor and club, but the student who does not study when the training is finished will never progress.

Aidan Trimble—Sixth Dan, Former World Karate Champion

Unarmed combat techniques are extremely physically challenging, and soldiers must train hard. They must be fit, flexible, strong, fast, and powerful. Just as importantly, they must be resilient and determined to win at all costs.

What Are
Special Forces?

Elite soldiers have been around for as long as armies and warfare. In ancient Persia (a territory in the Middle East that is now the country of Iran), there existed an elite corps of soldiers known as the Athanatoi, which means "Immortals." These were hand-picked warriors, experts with daggers and light bow and arrows.

Under the leadership of King Xerxes in 480 B.C., the Athanatoi helped win a major victory over the Greeks at Thermopylae, a mountainous pass along the eastern Greek coastline. Using stealth and speed, they moved quickly through the mountains above the Greek positions and attacked them from the rear, throwing the Greek forces into disarray.

The Greeks, however, had their own elite forces. In 331 B.C., Persia's opponent, Alexander the Great, the leader of a country called Macedonia in Greece, defeated the Persians at Guagamela in Persia using his special attack troops, the Companion Cavalry. These horseback-mounted fighters pretended to withdraw in order to draw the Persians into rocky, mountainous terrain where they could not use their chariots. Once the

A class of special forces soldiers practice front snap kicks. Asian soldiers usually learn either karate, taekwondo, judo, or kung fu, and many attain black-belt grade as part of their basic military training.

Persians fell into the trap, the Cavalry turned and attacked, inflicting terrible casualties. In this battle, 35,000 Macedonians defeated an army of 200,000 Persians.

ELITE FORCES FROM HISTORY

Other ancient civilizations had their own elite forces. In Britain during the time of Roman occupation (A.D. 43–409), many British tribes resisted the might of the Roman legions using special tactics. Boudicca, queen of the Britons, led one of the most powerful resistance armies. She was the leader of the Iceni tribe, a force of 100,000 Celtic warriors. Her warriors devastated Roman units using the guerrilla-warfare tactic of attack and run.

From the medieval period (A.D. 5th–15th century) onwards, elite forces grew around royal courts and became increasingly powerful and important. In Japan, by the 16th century, the infamous samurai had gone from simple tribal warriors and bodyguards to being the dominant class. They achieved this rise in power in part through their fearsome skills with the sword and bow, which remain unparalleled in history.

In the 15th and 16th centuries, the European country of Switzerland became a feared military presence because of its elite **Pikemen**, special soldiers trained to wield 15-foot-long (5-m) pikes in tight formations.

All the elite soldiers so far described fought as part of the regular army on the battlefield. Today, we have elite units that operate far away from large-scale forces, using only their weapons and unconventional tactics to survive. These real "special forces" were used for the first time (on a significant scale) in some of the early American wars.

U.S. Marines make a lap of an aircraft carrier during physical exercises. The Marines' basic training lasts for 12 weeks, and includes instruction in the U.S. Army's "Combatives" system of unarmed combat, as well as selected techniques from the world's martial arts.

Soviet special forces ("Spetsnaz") during a combat demonstration. Although not shown here, a unique part of Spetsnaz training is knife-throwing—the soldiers are trained to throw knives into targets at ranges of 30 ft (10 m) with considerable accuracy.

During the British wars against the French and the Native Americans in the mid-18th century, the British Army recruited a band of local woodsmen who became known as Rogers' Rangers, after the name of their leader, Captain Robert Rogers. Rogers' Rangers were masters of surprise, stealth, and sudden attack. They would slip silently into enemy positions through woodland or across rivers—they would even use ice skates to cross frozen rivers at high speed. Once in the enemy's camp, they would attack suddenly and then disappear like ghosts into the countryside. The impact of Rogers' Rangers was so great that in 1756, Rogers was made commander-in-chief of an entire **corps** of Rangers and was given free reign to recruit men like himself to the corps.

The impact of Rogers' Rangers was not lost on U.S. commanders during the American Civil War (1861–1865). The Union Army created two regiments of **sharpshooters** in 1861. While the Confederate forces would line up in mass ranks to fire volleys of shots, the sharpshooters would stalk the enemy in small groups and pick off officers with accurate sniper fire.

The Confederacy also had its own special troops. Colonel John S. Mosby led the 43rd Virginia Cavalry between 1863 and 1865 in a territory of Virginia that included parts of Fauqier and

By pulling the enemy's right arm upwards during the throw, the defender not only knocks him off balance, but also prevents him from grabbing the Browning 9-mm pistol on his right hip.

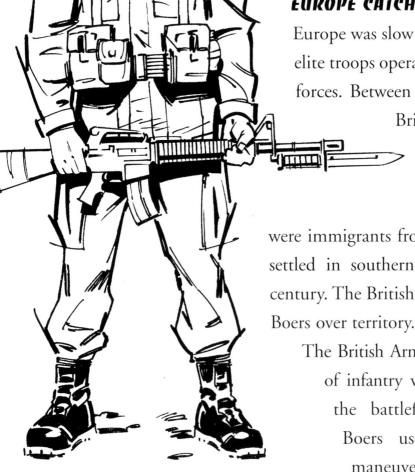

Loudoun counties. "Mosby's Raiders," as they came to be known, did not fight large battles. Instead, they rode horses and conducted lightning attacks against weak points in the Union's communications and supply chains.

EUROPE CATCHES UP

Europe was slow to take to the idea of elite troops operating away from main forces. Between 1880 and 1899, the British fought two wars in southern Africa known as the Boer Wars. The Boers were immigrants from Holland who had settled in southern Africa in the 17th century. The British went to war with the Boers over territory.

The British Army fought using ranks of infantry walking openly across the battlefield. However, the Boers used horses to out-maneuver the enemy, dug trenches to protect themselves, and applied accurate rifle fire to pick off

The M16A2 rifle's effective range of 1,829 ft (600 m) means unarmed combat is a last resort for this U.S. soldier.

the British soldiers one by one. In one terrible week of fighting, the British lost three battles, one after the other. Only when they began to use similar tactics and troops—usually hardy outdoorsmen from Australia, New Zealand, and Canada—did the British begin to gain the upper hand.

World War I (1914–1918) saw special forces introduced widely in Europe. Germany, in particular, began to experiment with a new form of soldier—the storm trooper. The **storm troopers** were special assault troops. They were trained to storm enemy trenches at high speed and to clear them out using hand grenades, explosives, flamethrowers, knives, and a new invention, the submachine gun. Under the leadership of Captain Willy Rohr, the storm troopers were used in several operations during battles in France and Russia with great success. After the war, the concept of the storm trooper lived on in the rise of Nazi Germany under Adolf Hitler, and entire legions of soldiers became known as storm troopers.

It was during World War II (1939–1945) that special forces as we know them today were born. Elite units were created to conduct daring operations behind enemy lines and to gather information, destroy vital targets, assassinate important people, and sabotage enemy industry. Germany produced the 800th Special Purpose Training Battalion Brandenburg, which was trained in all the special forces skills: assassination, survival, sabotage, foreign languages, communications, and intelligence gathering. The Italian navy created the Decima Flottiglia Mas (10th Light Flotilla) to conduct underwater sabotage operations against Allied ships.

The U.K. and U.S. formed secret service organizations known as the Special Operations Executive (SOE) and the Office of Strategic Services

Sniping is the total opposite to unarmed combat. Instead of fighting face-to-face, a sniper trains to take shots out to 4,573 ft (1,500 m). Even at this distance, the sniper will still expect to hit within 6 in (15 cm) of his aiming point.

(OSS), respectively. SOE agents were parachuted into German-occupied Europe, where they would pass themselves off as local civilians, using their fluency in foreign languages to gain vital information for the Allies. The OSS operated throughout Europe, the Middle East, and the Far East, and **infiltrated** reconnaissance soldiers around the beaches of Normandy, France, just before the Allied invasion of German-occupied Europe on June 6, 1944.

The most famous special forces unit to come out of World War II was the British Special Air Service (SAS). A daring and fearless British Army officer, Lieutenant David Stirling, created the SAS in 1941 during the British campaign against the Italian and German forces in North Africa. Stirling picked men as resilient as himself to attack enemy airfields deep within enemy lines. The SAS would drive onto enemy airfields in U.S.-made Willys jeeps mounted with machine guns and drive boldly down the runway, destroying the enemy aircraft with bullets and explosives. They became so feared by the enemy that they were known as the "ghosts of the desert." When the German and Italian forces were driven out of North Africa in 1943, the SAS went on to serve with distinction in Europe, fighting right up until the surrender of Germany in 1945.

MODERN SPECIAL FORCES

When World War II ended, most elite units, including the SAS, were disbanded. Without a war, most military leaders saw no use for these extraordinary troops. Two phenomena changed this. The first was that many European countries—particularly France, Britain, Portugal, and Belgium—found themselves fighting wars of independence in their overseas colonies. The second phenomenon was the Cold War. The Cold War was a state of hostility that existed between the Communist Soviet Union on one side and the democratic United States and their allies on the other. Though the hostility did not result in a major war between the two **superpowers**, many smaller wars were fought across the world.

Because of these smaller wars, special forces were once again needed. The European colonial powers needed them to fight against guerrilla forces using unconventional tactics, mainly in the Far East and Africa. The Cold War superpowers needed them to gather information about their enemies or to fight **covertly** in wars they were secretly sponsoring.

Britain formed the SAS once again in 1952 for action in the country of Malaya in the Far East. The Soviet Union created its elite Spetsnaz units in the 1950s. During the Vietnam War (1963–1975), the U.S. formed elite units to fight in the jungles of Vietnam against Communist soldiers. These included the Long Range Reconnaissance Patrol (LRRP), the 5th Special

Forces Group, and the U.S. Navy Sea Air Land (SEAL) units. After the war, in 1987, all U.S. special forces were brought under the control of one organization, the U.S. Special Operations Command.

In the 1970s and 1980s, elite forces were required to fight another enemy: terrorism. During these two decades, the number of terrorist organizations expanded rapidly. By the late 1980s, over 800 such groups were known to exist. Terrorist methods were mainly bombings, shootings, and assassinations, and they were horribly effective. Between 1970 and 1984, over 41,000 people were killed and 24,000 wounded in terrorist attacks around the world. The recent destruction of the World Trade Center in New York City is a continuation of the terrorists' attempts to bring disorder and chaos.

To combat this threat, specialized antiterrorist units were formed by many nations. The U.S. created the 1st Special Forces Operational Detachment Delta (commonly known as "Delta Force"); the British formed the Counter-Revolutionary Warfare (CRW) wing of the SAS; France established its Groupe d'Intervention Gendarmerie Nationale (GIGN) troopers; and Israel created the Sayeret Mat'kal organization. These units, and many others like them across the world, are trained to fight terrorists at their own game.

Terrorists are difficult to find and fight. In the late 1980s, only a tenth of terrorists were captured or killed. However, the elite forces have had some major successes. The war against terrorists in Afghanistan has demonstrated that those who perpetrate terrorist outrages will have few hiding places.

Modern special forces are usually the first troops to enter war zones. They are masters of weapons, communications, **surveillance**, and combat. They are also deadly using only their bare hands, as they are trained in the arts of military unarmed combat.

OFFICERS IN DELTA FORCE

For officers to join Delta Force, there are some additional requirements. These are:

- To be a captain or major in rank.
- To have a college degree (Bachelor of Arts or Bachelor of Science).
- To have a minimum of 12 months command experience.

ENTRY REQUIREMENTS FOR DELTA FORCE

Delta Force is the elite U.S. Army antiterrorism unit, and one of the most secretive elite units in the world. Since its creation in the late 1970s, it has performed in many risky operations worldwide, the most recent at the time of this writing being service against Taliban fighters in Afghanistan. Though the training for Delta Force is done in secret, the following are the entry requirements for recruits:

- All Delta troopers have to be volunteers. They must already be serving as active-duty soldiers or be members of the Army Reserve or National Guard.
- Delta troopers have to be male, U.S. citizens, and at least 22 years old.
- They must be airborne-qualified (parachute-trained), or they must volunteer for airborne training when recruited.
- Delta soldiers have a full security investigation into their background. If they have a civil or military criminal record, a record of disciplinary problems in the Army, or any previous membership in an inappropriate organization, they will be rejected.

• They must be very physically fit and have no physical limitations. Their health will be tested at an initial medical examination, which also tests their fitness for high-altitude parachuting and scuba diving.

• The initial physical qualification test involves numerous push-ups and sit-ups, a crawl across land of several hundred yards, a 2-mile (3.2-km) run, and a 109-yd (100-m) swim, all while wearing boots and military fatigues.

In subsequent training, Delta operatives are taught some distinctive skills. These include driving locomotives, hot-wiring cars and trucks (starting the engine without keys), lock-picking, negotiation, foreign languages, and skiing. In addition, they are pushed to their physical limits in excruciating physical training exercises—about 80 percent of the people who attempt Delta training do not make it through to the end.

During the Gulf War (1990–1991), Delta Force operators roamed behind enemy lines in heavily armed four-wheel-drive buggies known as Fast Attack Vehicles (FAVs), blowing up Iraqi Scud missile launchers. At present in Afghanistan, Delta Force troops are hard at work flushing out Taliban and Al Qaeda fighters in the mountains of Afghanistan using stealth and firepower.

The talents of elite units like Delta Force means that many nations rely heavily on them to win today's conflicts. They are also the most discrete warriors, fighting the enemy stealthily and efficiently using, among other things, unarmed combat. In the hands of elite soldiers, unarmed combat is a tool for disposing of the enemy brutally and silently. Their training involves looking through the repertoires of all the world's martial arts and selecting only the most deadly and effective techniques to take into action.

UPPER CUT

A soldier performs a traditional boxer's uppercut, striking the enemy beneath the chin. At the moment of impact, the attacker pushes up with his knees, thereby transferring all his body weight into the punch.

Military Unarmed Combat

The earliest evidence of advanced unarmed combat techniques comes from the Middle East. A copper ornament found in Babylonia (an ancient Middle Eastern territory) dating back to 3000 B.C. shows two men locked in a wrestling fight, gripping each other's belts as in the Japanese Sumo style of fighting. In Egypt, paintings on the walls at Beni-Hasan, a village in the east of the country on the Nile River, dated 3400 B.C., shows fighters throwing one another.

Wrestling seems to be the oldest of all forms of unarmed combat. In ancient Greece and Rome, wrestling became a popular, if violent, sport. Greece had a form of wrestling known as the **pancratium**, in which submission or death were the only results. In Rome, the infamous gladiators often conducted wrestling matches in addition to their battles with swords. The Emperor Commodus (the villain of the recent Hollywood film *Gladiator*), who reigned between A.D. 180 and 192, was an expert wrestler who won over 500 bouts.

In Britain, wrestling was part of the Tailtin Games, a yearly festival that was first held in 1829 B.C. and ran until A.D. 554. (British wrestling

Two Spetsnaz soldiers fight during unarmed combat training. In elite Russian units such as the Naval Infantry, up to 40 percent of the entire physical training program is taken up with wrestling, martial arts, knife fighting, and bayonet drills.

included kicking people on the shins while wearing horseshoes attached to ordinary footwear!) In Japan, wrestling was established as a martial art by at least 23 B.C., when the name of the champion fighter Sukune first appears in ancient writings.

VIOLENT TIMES

The examples of ancient wrestling mentioned relate more to sport and competition than to military unarmed combat. Their existence in these ancient times does show, however, that martial arts and fighting skills were important aspects of society. As trade routes developed between the Middle

Recruits to the elite British Parachute Regiment slug it out during an exercise known as "milling." They have to box each other without pausing for one minute, demonstrating courage and resilience rather than technique.

East and the Far East via northern India, these skills were shared between cultures and, eventually, armies.

Pure unarmed combat skills were most highly developed in ancient India and China. For most of their early history, China and India were not single countries; rather, they were collections of independent states. Territorial wars between these states were common. Each state needed tough individuals who could act as bodyguards or warriors to protect leaders or trade convoys passing through the dangerous, bandit-ridden countryside.

Unarmed combat skills became a necessity in these violent times and were practiced by commoner and nobility alike. The mythical Indian figure Agastiya advised all members of the warrior classes to learn unarmed combat. Hence, many temples around India have stone carvings of gods and men fighting using martial arts techniques. The unarmed combat skills of China and India were eventually written down in the 3rd century A.D. These writings became the foundations for the martial arts as we know them today.

MARTIAL ARTS TRADITIONS IN JAPAN

Japan soon created its own martial arts traditions and skills. The most famous Japanese fighters were the samurai and the ninja. The samurai were an elite fighting force created by the Japanese government in the mid-eighth century. Their job was to protect the interests of the royal court, and so they were highly trained in fighting with swords, bow and arrows, and their fists and feet.

The samurai gained a reputation for invincibility and ferocity on the battlefield, and their influence in Japan steadily grew. By the 15th and 16th centuries, the samurai effectively ruled the land, and the central government

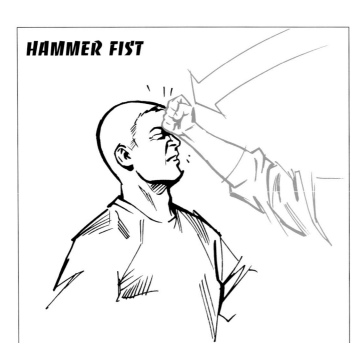

HAMMER FIST

The hammer fist uses the base of the fist as a weapon. The fist is brought down in a "hammer" action onto an exposed target, usually the bridge of the nose or the collarbone. The fist must be kept tight to avoid a broken little finger on impact.

collapsed. Japan was divided up into territories ruled by local masters called shoguns. A samurai would be loyal to his local shogun and he would fight other samurai in lethal battles for supremacy.

The ninja were also born during this time. They were originally either peasants who refused to serve the samurai masters or former samurai themselves whose lord had been killed. They gathered in secret locations in the mountainous Iga and Koga regions of Japan, and became an elite band of saboteurs and assassins who could be hired by anybody who could afford them. They had impressive unarmed combat skills, which they used to dispose of sentries (soldiers who guarded the gates) or assassinate enemy leaders. Their martial art, known as **ninjutsu**, contained a fearsome repertory of nerve strikes, strangles, neck breaks, and lethal punches and kicks.

The samurai and the ninja declined in power in the 16th century, when the ruler Tokugawa Ieyasu (1542–1616) ascended to the throne. He unified Japan as a country, and there followed three centuries of peace. With no

A Korean special forces soldier demonstrates a spectacular aikido throw on a colleague. All special forces of the Republic of Korea must attain a black belt in either taekwondo or another martial art to pass through the basic training program.

wars to fight, the ninja and samurai had no employment. Slowly, their skills deteriorated, and they steadily disappeared from Japanese society.

MODERN MILITARY UNARMED COMBAT

Many miles away from China and Japan, Europe had less of a military unarmed combat tradition. Its armies tended to focus on swordsmanship for the most part (although there are several British and French medieval texts with illustrations of unarmed combat techniques). In more modern times, the increase in the power and availability of weapons, particularly firearms, led to a worldwide decrease in the military use of unarmed combat. By the early 20th century, when most soldiers went into battle with rifles supported by long-range artillery, unarmed combat was rarely taught (apart from a few basic techniques). The soldiers of World War I would have received almost no unarmed combat training at all—except that which other soldiers passed on to them from experience.

Then, in the early 1940s, matters started to change. Japanese and Chinese forces began to receive basic instruction in **kung fu** or **karate** techniques to use in battle. In Western armies, the creation of special forces units led to an increased interest in unarmed combat. Special forces operations often require the silent disposal of opponents, or at least the physical means to continue fighting even when ammunition has run out. Certain individuals took it upon themselves to teach lethal unarmed combat to this new breed of soldier. Two of the most important teachers of these techniques were U.S. Army Colonel Rex Applegate and British Army Captain William Ewart Fairburn.

Applegate (1914–1998) was a tough hunter and marksman who, during the war, found himself assigned to the 209th Military Police Company. He

THE BIRTH OF KARATE

One interesting legacy of the samurai period was the birth of karate, the cornerstone for many modern military martial arts. In the 15th century, Japanese warlords occupied the island of Okinawa off the Japanese coast. They forbade any islander to carry weapons, as these were seen as a mark of nobility and thus a threat to the occupiers. In response, the islanders created a way of fighting without weapons. It relied on fast and powerful blocks, kicks, and punches to defeat an opponent. This became known as karate, a Japanese word that is translated as "empty hand." Today, karate is the most practiced martial art in the world.

was a large man who had learned a lot about unarmed combat from his policeman father. By 1942, Applegate's talents in unarmed combat had been spotted, and he was reassigned to the OSS to train special operatives in hand-to-hand fighting. He taught the agents only those techniques that would seriously injure or kill any opponent, no matter what his size. After the war, he went on to become an unarmed combat consultant to several armies and police forces around the world. He wrote three influential books, one of which is called *Kill or Get Killed*. This book is used today as an official U.S. Marine combat training manual.

Captain Fairburn taught a similar style of combat to that of Applegate. He was responsible for training British commandos and the SOE, as well as U.S. agents of the OSS. One of his students, George Langelaan, wrote of

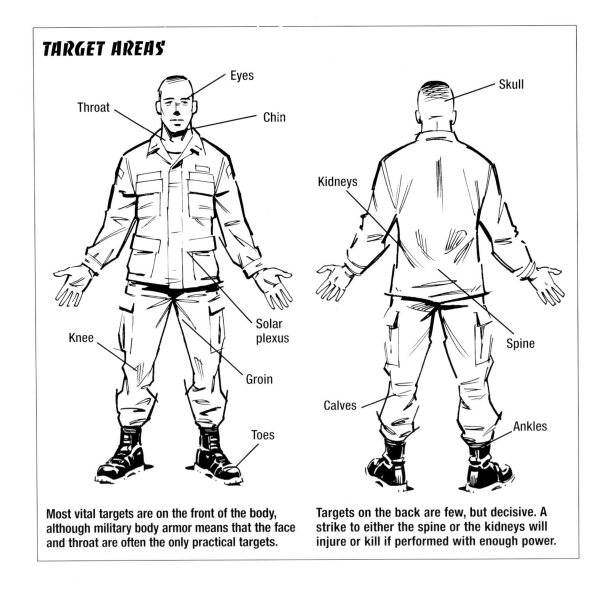

TARGET AREAS

Eyes

Throat

Chin

Skull

Kidneys

Knee

Solar plexus

Spine

Groin

Calves

Toes

Ankles

Most vital targets are on the front of the body, although military body armor means that the face and throat are often the only practical targets.

Targets on the back are few, but decisive. A strike to either the spine or the kidneys will injure or kill if performed with enough power.

the experience: "By the time we finished our training, I would have willingly tackled any man, whatever his strength, size, or ability. He taught us to face the possibility of a fight without the slightest tremor of apprehension."

After World War II, many armies took the lessons of Applegate and Fairburn into their training. Today, all soldiers receive unarmed combat instruction as part of their basic training. The standard of instruction can vary, however. Some soldiers will receive just a few sessions, whereas others will become world-class fighters. The individuals who become experts are usually members of special forces or the fortunate members of those armies that recognize the value of unarmed combat skills.

Nations that invest heavily in unarmed combat training include Korea, which trains all its soldiers in a special martial art called tukong moosul; and Russia, which instructs its special forces in a unique martial art called combat sambo. Israel is another nation that has invested heavily in unarmed combat training; its system is called krav maga. All men and women trained in these combat methods are lethal using only their bare hands.

KRAV MAGA

Israel has one of the few armies in which everyone is trained in unarmed combat to a high level. Modern Israel was created as a Jewish homeland in 1948 out of the British territory called Palestine. It has been fighting against Arab opponents for almost all of its existence, and its soldiers have seen more combat than almost any other army in the world since World War II. Because of its warrior history, Israel has developed a good unarmed combat system, called krav maga. This combat system is so successful that not only is it taught to the entire Israeli Army; it is also taught to the FBI, the U.S. Army, and to the New York Police Department. It is also taught to elite forces worldwide.

Krav maga was invented by a man named Imi Lichtenfeld. Lichtenfeld was born in 1901 in Czechoslovakia. His father was a circus acrobat, a wrestler, and later, a policeman. Lichtenfeld himself became interested in combat sports and wrestled at a professional level. Soon, the skills he learned were put to the test. In the 1930s in Europe, **anti-Semitism** became widespread in Germany, Austria, and Czechoslovakia, and Lichtenfeld found himself fighting against gangs of **fascist** youths. Lichtenfeld eventually left Czechoslovakia and settled in Israel. There, he began to teach his unarmed combat methods to Israeli soldiers.

The krav maga system illustrates perfectly the difference between military unarmed combat and the martial arts taught to most civilians. Martial arts such as karate, aikido, taekwondo, and judo usually feature sophisticated philosophies. Most of these philosophies stem from the Eastern religions of Buddhism and Taoism, which emphasize using peaceful methods to resolve fights before turning to violence. The martial arts also tend to have competitive or sporting versions.

Military unarmed combat is quite different. It has no rules, no philosophy, no sporting version, and only one aim: to kill or disable the enemy. Because it is designed for the life-or-death situations of war, every fighting technique must work—and work quickly. If military unarmed combat seems crude when compared to spectacular martial arts, it is because it is designed to do nothing more than win fights.

COMBAT SAMBO

Combat sambo is the lethal martial art taught to Russian special forces. It is made up of different ancient unarmed combat skills that were practiced in Russia by various clans and tribes until around the ninth century. Together, these ancient combat skills were simply known as Russian martial art (RMA). RMA was a fearsome fighting art, but by

CLUB ATTACK

The attacker lunges forward, bringing a club down towards his opponent's head in a violent hacking motion.

The defender blocks the attack at the opponent's elbow, stopping the club from gathering force and making contact.

the 17th century, the invention and widespread distribution of firearms meant that RMA was used less and less. It was, however, kept alive by various experts who practiced the techniques in their own homes and communities.

In 1917, a revolution in Russia brought RMA under Communist control. The Communist government ordered a man named Comrade Voroshilov to study all the remains of RMA and create from them a complete system of unarmed combat for the new Soviet Union. Voroshilov gathered 25 different RMA styles and mixed them together with karate, judo, kung fu, and various other martial arts. The result was the Soviet Close-Quarters Combat (CQC) program.

The CQC program consisted of several different levels of unarmed combat. At its most secret, it contained a range of lethal techniques that were only taught to elite undercover units. Regular military units learned a useful, but watered-down, version of CQC. Eventually, all CQC arts were called samozashchitya bez oruzhiya, or sambo for short.

Today, sambo exists in two basic military forms: combat sambo and combat sambo spetsnaz. Combat sambo is the form taught to all military units in Russia, and it is similar to the U.S. unarmed combat program. Combat sambo spetsnaz is the lethal techniques of the CQC program. It is taught to government agents, paratroopers, Marine units, and Spetsnaz special forces. Although some sambo schools have been created in the U.S., little is known about sambo's more lethal range of techniques.

TUKONG MOOSUL

Tukong moosul was created in the 1970s by the South Korean Army to counter the threat from its Communist neighbor, North Korea. Within this new tukong (special combat) unit were six martial arts masters; the unit's commander, General Change K. Oe, ordered them to develop a lethal fighting art unique to the team. It had to be the ultimate practical combat art, and was intended to have none of the weaknesses that some of the traditional martial arts displayed.

The result was tukong moosul, the last word simply meaning "martial arts." Tukong moosul, like krav maga, has no competition form—it is purely designed to kill and injure. In subsequent demonstrations of tukong moosul, South Korean military leaders were so impressed that today, parts of it are taught to all South Korean soldiers.

ELBOW STRIKE

Most unarmed combat actually takes place at a chest-to-chest distance of less than 2 ft (0.6 m). The elbow strike is an ideal technique for this range, being powerful, easy to use in confined spaces, and at the right position for a head attack.

Training to Fight

Soldiers must train hard to master unarmed combat techniques. Physically, they must be fit, flexible, strong, fast, and powerful. Mentally, they must be resilient and determined to win at all costs. These mental and physical abilities go hand in hand. Many martial artists are successful in the safety of the dojo, yet they fall apart mentally during real combat. Conversely, a fighter may be mentally tough, but if not physically fit, he or she will likely lose any fight lasting longer than 30 seconds.

THE TRAINING REGIME

Research has shown that most fights follow four stages:

1) The two opponents approach one another and prepare to do battle.
2) The fight begins with a burst of punches and kicks.
3) If the punches and kicks do not settle the fight immediately, the two opponents close up and grapple, usually on the floor.
4) One person submits or is defeated.

Researchers have found that this entire process from start to finish usually lasts no more than four to five seconds. However, the energy expended in

Soldiers practice "kihon"—basic martial arts techniques—during a training session. Once kihon are mastered, the students proceed to "kumite," which means actual fighting with a partner. Kihon and kumite are both Japanese terms.

those four to five seconds is equivalent to 20 minutes of high-impact exercise. If the fight goes on for more than 30 seconds, it is usually the fittest person who wins, regardless of fighting talent.

A STRONG BODY

Elite forces train their soldiers in two types of fitness: aerobic and anaerobic. Both types of training are essential for fighting endurance. Aerobic exercises increase the heart and breathing rate and sustain the increased rate over a period of time. This improves the body's capacity to transport oxygen around its **cardiovascular** system. The more oxygen circulating, the better the levels of endurance and stamina. Aerobic exercises include activities such as running, cycling, and **circuit** training. Without this sort of fitness, a soldier in a fight would quickly become tired, out of breath, and feel faint.

Anaerobic exercise does not require an increase of oxygen in the body. It usually describes activities that are meant to develop muscle tone and strength rather than stamina. Examples of anaerobic fitness include weight training, stretching, and many of the punching and kicking exercises of the martial arts.

Elite forces training is designed around both types of exercise. This type of training pushes the recruits to the limits of exhaustion. Military unarmed combat fitness training can be similar to that used in civilian martial arts clubs, but with some crucial differences. Civilian martial arts place a high emphasis on hip flexibility, to facilitate very high kicks. Military unarmed combat, however, does not develop such flexibility, because very high kicks are generally unsuitable for serious combat. A leg kicked very high can be caught easily, and while the person is kicking, he is off-balance. Elite forces

A U.S. soldier performs an expert block on a kick during unarmed combat training in the deserts of the Middle East. Unarmed combat rarely occurs in desert terrain, because the long visibility means that the enemy is engaged at great distance with weaponry.

train their soldiers only to kick to abdomen height and below. Kicks to these targets can be fast and difficult to catch.

Initial training in unarmed combat usually takes place in a gym or a training circle marked out on the floor. U.S. Army doctrine states that each pair of soldiers should have a space 8 ft (2.6 m) in diameter to practice unarmed combat effectively. Safety precautions are tight. Soldiers are required to empty their pockets and to remove jewelry, identification tags, and glasses before training.

At first, practice of the techniques is light and easy. As the soldiers become more and more familiar with the movements, the speed and power of the techniques is increased. Strikes to any vulnerable points must be pulled short to avoid serious injury, although the soldiers will also do a lot of work on punching bags to develop their power and spirit. If training

BREAK-FALL

STEP 1: The soldier begins to topple backwards and moves his arms out to the side in preparation.

STEP 2: As the soldier hits the floor, he rolls his legs backwards and slaps the floor to reduce the impact.

STEP 3: The bottom is raised to make the spine roll along the floor rather than smash into it.

STEP 4: The soldier rolls his feet back down to the floor to complete the break-fall.

FEROCIOUS TRAINING TECHNIQUES

Soviet Spetsnaz training involves particularly harsh exercises. A soldier must run through several rooms, fighting multiple opponents in each room and using blows that approach full power. The Spetsnaz consequently has a higher rate of injuries during training than almost any other elite force in the world. Similarly, at the end of Royal Marines training in Norway, gangs of instructors often attack recruits with potentially knock-out blows to see if they have the techniques and courage to survive.

with knives or **bayonets**, these will remain in their scabbards (sheaths) throughout training. Alternatively, rubber knives may be used. An interesting training technique involves coating a rubber knife with lipstick before training. If the soldier defending against the knife is caught with the blade, a red mark will show up.

Elite units introduce more innovative and ruthless training programs. Unarmed combat training is sometimes conducted in small rooms full of office equipment. This allows the soldier to actually see which techniques will work and which will not in real fighting environments (as opposed to familiar, open gym halls). Such training produces ultra-tough soldiers who are at home with unarmed fighting. The important point in unarmed combat training is that it must, at some point, actually become dangerous so that the soldiers get used to danger and become confident that they can handle themselves in dangerous situations.

SIT-UPS

STEP 1: Sit-ups are designed to provide the abdominal strength essential for powerful kicking and punching. From a sitting position, with hands behind head, the soldiers move to a full sitting position by tensing the stomach muscles.

SAS FITNESS AND COMBAT TRAINING

The SAS is a good example of a particularly tough training regime. The training program for recruits is 26 weeks long. The first 12 weeks are known as Selection Training and consist of a series of punishing physical exercises conducted in the Brecon Beacon Mountains in the country of Wales, U.K. The climax of the 12 weeks is the "endurance march," in which the recruits have to cover 40 miles (64.4 km) in 20 hours, carrying over 100 lb (45 kg) of kit (his equipment) and moving up and down steep mountains. (Kit usually consists of a large rucksack, web belt holding ammunition and utility pouches, and a rifle.) Those that survive this stage (about 80 percent drop out) will have developed an incredible aerobic fitness for fighting.

Actual unarmed combat instruction takes place during the next phase of recruitment, Continuation Training (CT). CT lasts for 14 weeks and teaches the soldiers the basic skills of an elite SAS soldier, including parachuting, survival, jungle warfare, hostage rescue, reconnaissance, and

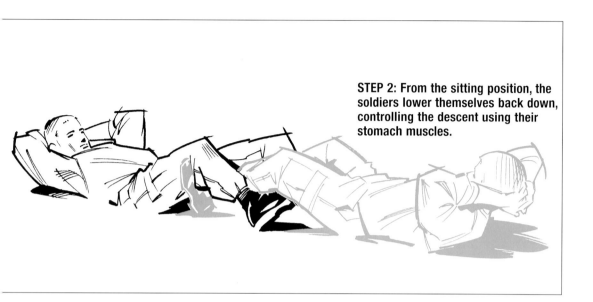

STEP 2: From the sitting position, the soldiers lower themselves back down, controlling the descent using their stomach muscles.

much more. Close-Quarter Battle (CBQ) training contains the unarmed combat instruction. CBQ was developed in the 1960s, and focuses on close-range killing with pistols, knives, submachine guns, and unarmed means.

The unarmed combat techniques taught to the SAS are simple, but deadly. They include lethal blows, strangulation moves, and ways of fighting using improvised weapons. Typical improvised weapons include rolled-up newspapers, which can be jabbed into an enemy's solar plexus or throat, and handfuls of coins, which can give extra weight to a punch.

A STRONG MIND

When an individual is faced with a fight, his or her body and mind go through several stages of automatic response. First, a part of the brain known as the **hypothalamus** triggers the release of two hormones, called adrenaline and noradrenaline, into the bloodstream. These hormones increase the breathing and heartbeat and pump blood to the muscles. This

STRIKING EQUIPMENT

Punchbags usually weigh between 44 lb (20 kg) and 66 lb (30 kg) and are used for developing power in punches and kicks.

The Makiwara is a 7–8 ft (2.2–2.6 m) plank used to train fast punching techniques.

response gives the person an enormous amount of energy to either fight or run away.

There is a problem with this automatic response, however. The "fight or flight" reaction is an ancient one in human beings and was designed for times when humans were constantly under threat from wild animals. Today, our lives are generally safe, so there is less of a need for this reaction response. Thus, when this response is triggered, we are often so unfamiliar with it that the strange sensations paralyze us with fear and confusion.

Whether someone freezes or fights often depends on his experience and training. The human mind is like a huge, complex computer. Every time we have a new experience, it is stored away in the brain, like a file. The next time we have the

THE MIND-BODY CONNECTION

Recently in the U.K., one group of people was asked to imagine doing weight training for 20 minutes each day, while another group actually performed 20 minutes of weight training each day. At the end of the week, it was found that both groups had achieved similar muscle development!

same type of experience, the brain pulls out the file and uses it to perform the task. If we meet an unfamiliar experience, the brain will use the file that matches the experience as closely as possible and create a new file from the results. When we practice one particular skill over and over again, such as throwing a basketball through a hoop, the repetition makes the file bigger and more detailed. Eventually, the body and mind become so familiar with a task that they start to perform it automatically, without conscious thought. For example, think about how difficult it was when you first learned to ride a bike. Chances are, now that you are more experienced, your "ride a bike" file is so advanced that you can just climb on and go without thinking.

It is this level of response that elite soldiers try to develop for unarmed combat. During training, the soldiers will practice their fighting as realistically as possible. For example, the soldier will train for unarmed combat in his or her uniform, not gym gear. Punches and kicks are thrown at full power—if the recipient does not block them or get out of the way, he or she will be hurt.

U.S. special forces practice fighting in rooms full of chairs and tables in order to familiarize themselves with real fighting environments. It is important that the training be both realistic and stressful. If it is realistic enough, the brain will be able to build up a "fight file," which allows the person to know in advance what a real fight will be like. If it is stressful enough, the soldier will become accustomed to the adrenal response and will always fight rather than freeze.

One interesting fact about the human mind is that often it cannot tell the difference between experience that is imagined and experience that is real. If something is imagined very vividly and realistically, then the brain will start to build up a file around that mental picture, which it will then use in real life. For this reason, athletes will often imagine themselves winning an event in order to improve their chances of actually

U.S. Army Rangers practice unarmed combat at training camp. The Rangers began intensive unarmed combat training during the Vietnam War, and used it to dispose of enemy troops silently during covert ambush missions.

DYNAMIC TENSION STRETCH

Dynamic tension stretching involves pulling against a partner while performing a stretch. The aim of this technique is not to pull each other over, but to hold the partner under tension to stretch their muscles more effectively.

doing so. Similarly, martial artists picture themselves performing a perfect kick, the result being that their kicks do improve.

More and more elite forces are starting to use "visualization" as a technique of training—the U.S. special forces in particular. They picture themselves performing perfect attacks and defenses in their minds' eyes, and so improve their actual performance. The secret to effective visualization is to picture the scene as vividly as possible, imagining every detail of color, sound, sight, shape, and sensation. Fully imagining the reality of unarmed combat helps the "file" to be ready for when real combat starts.

Attacking the Enemy

The type of unarmed combat taught to special forces is concerned with winning life-or-death battles. Therefore, every attacking technique must either injure or incapacitate—or even kill—the opponent. This chapter will look at some of these techniques. Please remember: the following descriptions and illustrations are for educational purposes only and are not meant as instruction.

BODY WEAPONS

The first lesson in military unarmed combat training is body weapons. The most versatile body weapon is the hand. When it is curled up tightly into a fist, it is used to hit the opponent as a punch, or strike in a chopping motion as a "hammer fist." A fist must be made correctly, or else the hand may be hurt upon contact with the target or, accidentally, the enemy's rifle or a heavy ammunition pouch.

When making a proper fist, the fingers are first curled tightly into the palm of the hand and the thumb is placed well underneath, on the outside of the fingers. The striking surface when punching is the first (largest) two knuckles. To avoid damaging the wrist when hitting, the bones of the back

Left: Russian Spetsnaz training is particularly brutal, and punches and kicks are often delivered at full power. Consequently, Spetsnaz has the highest percentage of injuries and fatalities of any special forces unit during training.

READY STANCE

The ready stance protects the soldier from frontal attack while allowing him to respond with a variety of punches and kicks.

of the hand are held parallel to and in line with the top of the forearm. For the hammer fist, the striking point is the fleshy part of the hand between the wrist and the first joint of the little finger (anywhere else will usually result in a broken wrist or knuckle joint). Russian Spetsnaz soldiers regularly smash wooden boards and concrete blocks to test their fist construction, as well as their power. If they make a fist correctly, the target will shatter; if it is made incorrectly, however, the result will be multiple hand fractures.

The fist is only one of the weapons that the hand offers. The fingers are also used; they can poke at soft targets, such as the eyes, and they can grip or scratch. A hand can also be held open and rigid like a knife and used for "karate chop" strikes to the enemy's throat and neck. Further up the arm, the elbow is a powerful weapon for short-range attacking. The special forces in Thailand commonly use the elbow when engaging in the art of muay thai (kickboxing). This is because muay thai training fights are often conducted at close quarters, and

"Breaking" is the practice of smashing wooden boards or concrete blocks to test power. Recent world records for breaking include 5,000 wooden boards shattered in seven hours and 40 concrete slabs broken with one blow.

it is easier to apply an elbow at these ranges than a punch. The elbow can be swung at or dug into an opponent's torso or head. It can generate a lot of force because it is such a hard surface, and it carries more body weight behind it than a fist.

The feet and knees are the other two main body weapons. The feet are used for kicking and for stamping attacks to the opponent's feet, shins, knees, or against other parts of his or her body if the opponent is on the ground. Whereas stamping is a natural action, combat kicking is not, and thus a lot of practice is needed before it will be useful in action. The knees are like the elbows: good for close-range combat. They can be thrust upwards into the enemy's groin or abdomen or bashed into his or her kneecap or thigh.

These are the main body weapons that a soldier will use in combat. Several others exist, but they are often impractical for military unarmed

A group of soldiers watch a demonstration of an elbow strike. The instructor has trapped his opponent's left arm with his elbow. This will allow him to pull the opponent to the ground after delivering the elbow strike.

BASIC PUNCHES

STEP 1: The soldier prepares to punch with the right fist, extending the opposite fist (the "reaction hand") out in front and holding the punching fist palm-up.

STEP 2: When punching, the reaction hand is pulled back as the punch goes forward. This puts more power into the punch. The punching fist is twisted palm-down upon impact.

combat. Head butts, for example, are dangerous to use against other soldiers who are wearing helmets. Soldiers can be taught to bite their opponents if the situation is serious enough, but as this act carries the danger of catching blood-borne diseases, it is usually avoided.

THUMPING AND DUMPING

The U.S. Army's unarmed combat manual instructs the soldier to use every means possible to hit vital points and end the fight. It uses the phrase "thump him and dump him" as a memory aid. What is important is that each attack is launched with total commitment and with all the power the soldier can muster.

VITAL POINTS

The object of military unarmed combat is to attack the enemy soldier's weak points using the body weapons or any improvised weapons at hand. The human body has many points that are particularly vulnerable to attack; that is, those points that are not covered with protective muscle or bone. They include places where there are exposed groups of nerves (the solar plexus and groin); joints that can be twisted, locked, or damaged (the elbows and knees); or fleshy body parts that are vulnerable to deep, penetrating strikes (the eyes and kidneys). A soldier's opponents are likely to be other soldiers who are fit, strong, and also trained in unarmed combat. Therefore, he or she will only target those points on the enemy's body that will end a fight quickly.

THE ATTACK

A soldier begins an attack by closing the distance between him- or herself and his or her opponent, which involves nimble footwork. The soldier stands with his or her feet shoulder-width apart and one leg extended out in front of the body, so that he or she faces the opponent at a 45-degree angle. The arms are held up loosely to protect the body and the sides of the head. This is known as the "ready" stance. When moving forward, the soldier pushes off his or her back leg while moving his or her front leg forward, then draws his or her back leg up to form the original ready position. When moving backwards, the action is reversed, pushing backwards with the front leg, and so on. This method of moving stops the soldier from crossing his or her legs and becoming unbalanced, and offers a good platform for springing into a powerful attack.

The soldier's movements should put him or her within long, medium, or close range of his or her opponent, depending on how he or she wants to attack. At long range, only the legs can be used to kick the opponent. At medium

FRONT KICK

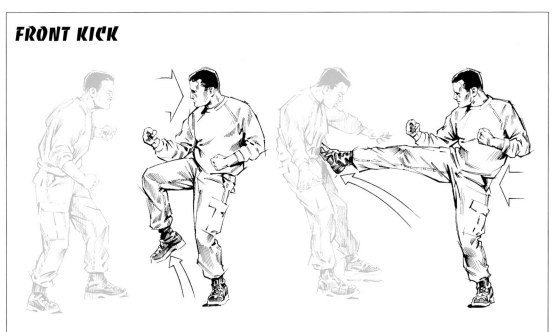

STEP 1: The knee is lifted high in preparation for the kick, a measure which prevents the kick from becoming snagged on anything as it powers forward.

STEP 2: As the kick goes in, the attacker thrusts his hips forward and transfers all of his body weight into the attack.

KNEE STRIKE

In real unarmed combat, very few kicks are directed above the waist. A knee strike allows the attacker to disable his opponent without losing his balance or exposing the kicking leg to being caught and held.

range, the soldier is able to use kicks, punches, or strikes. At close range, only short hook punches, grapples, or knee and elbow strikes are used. Ideally, the soldier should attack at all three ranges as he or she closes in, stopping the enemy from responding at any point. A typical attack would be a kick to the groin (long range), then a punch to the face or throat (medium range), then a stranglehold around the enemy's neck (short range).

PUNCHES

There are four basic types of punches: the jab, the hook, the uppercut, and the reverse punch. The jab involves thrusting the fist of the front hand straight ahead to the target. This punch is quick, but has limited power; it is often used to stun the opponent before a heavier blow is delivered. A hook punch is a classic boxer's "haymaker" punch. It swings in a wide arc, hitting the target from the side rather than the front, and carries with it a lot of power from the shoulder. The uppercut uses a similar technique, but the fist swings upwards to connect underneath the target. It is usually used to hit beneath the chin for a knockout blow. The reverse punch is the most powerful type of punch. If the soldier is standing with his or her left foot forward and his or her right foot back, then the punch is made with the right hand. The fist is thrust at the target; when

WIN AT ALL COSTS

Unlike many martial arts, military unarmed combat goes by the philosophy of "win at all costs." Techniques that might appear harsh in the civilian world are accepted in military combat simply because of the different circumstances—staying alive might depend upon their use. Soldiers are trained to use whatever is at hand to defend themselves in unarmed combat, including pens, chairs, and heavy ashtrays—anything that can be turned into a weapon. Military unarmed combat instructors are looking for men and women who will not fight by the rules, but will use every deception and improvised weapon available to win the fight.

it makes contact, the right hip is pushed forward hard. This action has the effect of transferring all the soldier's body weight into the punch, thus maximizing its destructive impact on the target. A soldier might only weigh 140 lb (64 kg), but if he or she can generate a 140-pound-punch, then he or she will be able to cause considerable damage.

Whichever type of punch is used, certain rules of technique always apply. The arm should be as relaxed as possible when the fist is traveling forward. This will make the punch fast, as relaxed muscle contracts and expands much more quickly than tense muscle. When the target is hit, however, the whole body should be tensed hard in order to deliver the entire body weight into the contact.

The U.S. Army's unarmed combat manual also teaches the "hit and stick" principle. According to this principle, when the target is hit, the soldier should leave his or her fist there for at least a tenth of a second. This is enough time for all the energy of the punch to go into the target and cause maximum damage. If the punch is snatched away as soon as it touches the target, it will have little effect.

KICKS

Kicking is an advanced skill that takes practice to perfect. Soldiers usually learn three kicks: the front kick, the side kick, and the roundhouse kick. The front kick is similar to the action of kicking a ball, the difference being that the hips are thrust forward when the foot connects, to impart maximum power.

This is a fast and powerful kick. It is easy to perform and is excellent for quick, hard strikes to the shins, knees, and groin. When performing the

HEAD-BUTT ATTACK

STEP 1: A soldier is grabbed from behind by an enemy who applies a chokehold. In response, he rocks his head forward.

STEP 2: He then drives it backwards into the enemy's face to break the hold. The target point is the enemy's nose.

side kick, the knee of the kicking leg is lifted high to the front, but then the leg is thrust out to the side of the body in a forceful pushing action. A side kick is used to drive an opponent away or to attack a vulnerable joint, such as the knee. Finally, the roundhouse kick involves spinning the body through 90 degrees and kicking in a slicing motion into the side of the target. The roundhouse kick is used to perform rapid attacks to the knees, thighs, and abdomen.

A soldier using kicks has to be cautious. Unless he or she is an exceptional kicker, such as the soldiers in the Korean and Thai special forces, all kicks should be aimed low and performed at a fast speed. If a soldier kicks above the waist and the kick is slow, his or her leg will be caught by the attacker. To avoid this danger, he or she should retract his or her kicking leg as fast as it went out. Similarly, if fighting in a building or in the woods, he or she must take care that the kick does not catch on an object as it moves toward the target.

VULNERABLE POINTS IN UNARMED COMBAT

The following body parts are particularly vulnerable to injury during unarmed combat:

• Eyes. These are struck with the fingers to blind the opponent. Attacks have to be fast, as the eyes are well protected by the blinking and head-movement reflexes.

• Temples. The temples have a weak covering of bone and feature a large artery and a cluster of nerves. Hitting here can knock the enemy out or even cause death.

• Nose. A quick punch to the nose will set the enemy's eyes watering. This will interfere with his or her vision and will leave him or her vulnerable to other attacks.

• Jaw and chin. The jaw and chin contain many nerve clusters. Hitting the point of the chin or side of the jaw can break or dislocate the jaw or knock the person unconscious.

• Neck and throat. This is one of the most dangerous areas to strike your opponent. A punch to the throat can cause the windpipe to collapse, resulting in suffocation. A hard strike to the side of the neck can damage vital arteries, veins, and nerves, and can cause the enemy's unconsciousness or death.

• Solar plexus. This is the soft part of the chest in the center of the ribcage. A strike here "winds" the enemy and can even cause unconsciousness and death by rupturing internal organs.

• Floating ribs. These are the bottom ribs. They are called "floating" because they are not attached to the rib cage and so are easily bent inwards by a punch or kick. A strike here will result in severe pain, a damaged liver, or a punctured lung.

• Kidneys. The kidney areas are situated in the lower back on either side of the spine. There is little muscle covering here, and so a punch can cause unconsciousness, internal bleeding, or even death.

• Groin. In both men and women, the groin is quite sensitive to pain. In men, however, even a light strike to the testicles can result in debilitating pain or unconsciousness.

• Thigh. Kicking the outside of the thigh hard will numb the leg and affect the enemy's ability to move and fight.

• Knee. A hard kick to the knee can break the kneecap or damage the joint.

• Feet. Stamping on the feet can break the enemy's toes or the bones that run across the top of the foot.

Defensive Tactics

In any fight, it is well known that the first person who attacks is often the victor. This lesson also applies to unarmed combat. As most fights only last about four or five seconds, the first few blows that connect with vital targets will usually decide the fight.

It is an old military adage that "the best form of defense is attack," but it is true. During the recent war in the European country of Kosovo, U.S. Marines were deployed as peacekeeping troops. One day, a group of Marines ended up in a firefight with enemy forces that left several of the enemy dead and wounded. During a press conference after the event, a journalist asked a U.S. Marine officer whether it was true that the Marines had fired first, implying that it was they who had sparked the incident. The officer simply replied, "I hope so."

The point that the officer was making was that the soldier needs to ensure that it is he or she who delivers the first blows. When fighting elite opponents, however, that is not always possible. It is then that a soldier must rely on techniques of avoidance, blocking, and countering.

DEFENSIVE AWARENESS

Good defense starts with awareness of all the enemy's body movements.

Russian soldiers train in defensive techniques in winter snows. Russia has a long history of wrestling, and the techniques of wrestling filtered into the lethal Russian military martial art known as combat sambo.

A Russian special forces trooper defends against attack using a wrist lock. The knife shown is actually a bayonet for a Kalashnikov assault rifle. This features a serrated back edge, a razor-sharp cutting edge, and a special fitting for using the bayonet as a wire cutter.

Most people, soldiers included, make small signs with their body indicating that they are about to launch an attack. Soldiers and martial artists know this phenomenon as "telegraphing." Reading **telegraphed** movements helps the soldier make a quick and intelligent defense. Punches and kicks are usually telegraphed by the enemy's preparation, if he or she is unskilled. For example, a fist may be pulled backwards slightly before being thrown as a punch; when this happens, the person is, in effect, "cocking" his or her fist, ready to fire. Similarly, the enemy may signal that he or she is about to kick the defender by dropping his or her eyes at the intended target area or by fidgeting on the spot for a brief second while he or she figures out the range.

The defender must watch the enemy's entire body simultaneously for signals of an attack. The best way to do this is to focus his or her gaze on the solar plexus in the center of the chest. By staring at this point, the defender will become completely aware of the enemy's body movements through his or her peripheral vision. He or she should be particularly aware of movement in the elbows and knees. These body parts move more slowly than the feet and fists they power, so they are a good signal that an attack is coming.

DEFENDING FROM A PRONE POSITION

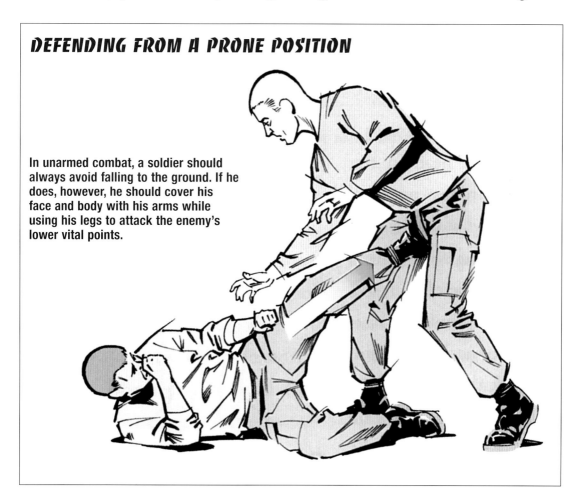

In unarmed combat, a soldier should always avoid falling to the ground. If he does, however, he should cover his face and body with his arms while using his legs to attack the enemy's lower vital points.

AVOIDANCE

The best form of defense against any attack is avoidance. Put simply, the defender should move his or her body so that all attacks simply miss. For punches to the face, there are two main avoidance techniques: the duck and the weave. The duck involves suddenly bending the knees to reduce height

Defense is always a preparation for an attack. Here, Russian soldiers do both simultaneously, blocking a punch with one hand while at the same instant delivering a punch with the right hand.

FOREARM BLOCKS

The forearm is the most useful blocking tool for defensive techniques. It can be swiped across the body and face to deflect punches from any direction and can even be used as a weapon if brought against the side of an opponent's head.

LIMBS OF STEEL

Some Korean unarmed combat specialists attain such durable limbs that a baseball bat can be broken across their arms without doing any physical damage. Soldiers trained in Thai boxing condition their legs by kicking cord-covered stakes or rubbing bottles up and down their shins until the skin is totally hardened. Do not attempt any of these conditioning exercises at home, as they can result in nerve damage to the limbs.

while dipping forward from the waist and pulling the head down into the shoulders. The three elements of this defense, performed simultaneously and with correct timing, should allow the defender to duck under the punch, then rise quickly with an uppercut punch as a counterattack.

The weave involves the defender snatching his or her upper body and head out of the way of the punch, moving either to the left or the right or rocking backwards out of the punch's range. The power for this movement comes from the waist and shoulders (not the head and neck), and it must be done with bent knees; the body is less flexible when the knees are stiff.

When avoiding kicks or punches to the body, sidestepping is the best measure. Sidestepping means just what it says: the defender steps quickly to the side as an attack is coming in so that it misses. Again, the knees need to be bent, for the required speed comes from pushing off with one leg to propel the body in the required direction. The soldier practices this maneuver without jumping too far away from his or her opponent. If he or she jumps completely out of reach of the enemy, he or she will have trouble counterattacking. The idea is to aim for just enough movement to allow the attack to miss, but to remain close enough so that it is possible to hit back using lots of power.

BLOCKING

Blocking punches and kicks is not as easy as it appears in the movies. Being hit with a heavy punch on the arm may knock the soldier off balance and leave him or her with a numb arm that is useless for fighting. To toughen up, soldiers do various "conditioning" exercises that harden the skin and deaden the pain response in particular areas of the body. For blocking conditioning, soldiers will take a partner and practice striking their forearms against each other for long periods of time, gradually increasing the intensity of the blows so that they adjust to the pain.

Blocking punches involves intercepting them and then guiding them away from the face or body. This skill requires great speed and judgment. The arms should be held up in the ready position so that an attack can be "swiped" away from any angle. The blocking surface is the forearm.

When blocking a jab or reverse punch, the defender intercepts the punching arm as closely to the wrist as possible, pushes it away from his or her face, then immediately counterattacks with his or her free hand. For a hook punch, both arms are used to block, one stopping the punch at the wrist, the other at the elbow. From here, the wrist can be gripped and the punching arm pulled straight; the hand that blocked at the elbow then delivers a chop to the enemy's exposed throat.

DOUBLE-HANDED BLOCK AGAINST A CLUB

The trick to blocking a club attack is to get as close to the enemy's body as possible—the further away the greater the speed and power of the strike.

Blocking kicks is more difficult, and so avoidance is always the preferred technique. The best moment to stop a kick is when it is just starting and gathering power. An excellent technique is to stop the kick as it begins by stamping at the ankle as it comes forward.

With enough practice, stopping a kick can be as simple as lifting the foot. This method also has the advantage of not hurting the defender, who is wearing strong army boots. A more courageous blocking technique for kicks is the X-block. In this technique, an X shape is made by crossing the arms at the wrists; the kick then gets trapped in the X as it comes forward. The X-block is best made against the attacker's knee before the foot flicks out into the kick, but even then it is a dangerous maneuver. The best policy of dealing with kicks and punches remains moving out of their way.

DEFENDING AGAINST A KNIFE ATTACK

Although civilian martial artists may encounter attackers with weapons, for military men and women, the use of weapons by the enemy is a near certainty. Obviously, unarmed combat is no defense against bullets and bombs, but it can be used against attackers with knives.

BLOCK-AND-THROW SEQUENCE

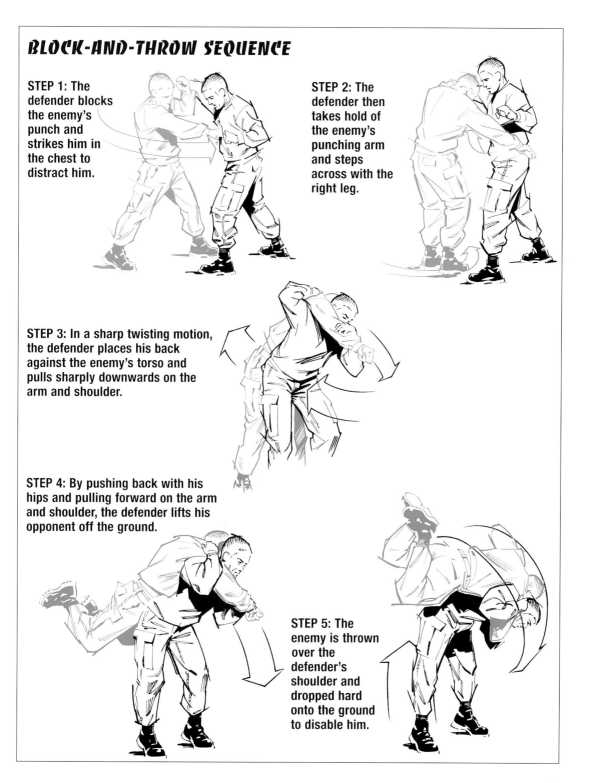

STEP 1: The defender blocks the enemy's punch and strikes him in the chest to distract him.

STEP 2: The defender then takes hold of the enemy's punching arm and steps across with the right leg.

STEP 3: In a sharp twisting motion, the defender places his back against the enemy's torso and pulls sharply downwards on the arm and shoulder.

STEP 4: By pushing back with his hips and pulling forward on the arm and shoulder, the defender lifts his opponent off the ground.

STEP 5: The enemy is thrown over the defender's shoulder and dropped hard onto the ground to disable him.

DEFENDING AGAINST A KNIFE ATTACK

STEP 1: Here, a soldier defends against a knife attack by grabbing the attacker's knife hand and stepping sharply across the left.

STEP 2: He then throws his attacker over his hip. Note how he always keeps control of the knife throughout.

Studies conducted by the Los Angeles Police Department showed that at close ranges, a knife is actually a more dangerous weapon than a gun. It can stab repeatedly and never runs out of ammunition. Traditional blocks against punches are useless against knives. Blocking a knife attack with a forearm is likely to result in a severe, even fatal, cut to the arm. Furthermore, a soldier's combat knife will be both a stabbing and a slashing weapon, and every time it touches a soldier, it will usually cause injury.

If a soldier is fighting against a knife-armed opponent, his or her best policy is to disable the opponent as quickly as possible while limiting the movement of the enemy's hand that is holding the knife. As the knife comes in, the defender can block the knife arm using a two-handed block, like the one described for blocking a hook punch. The hand that blocks at the wrist can then grab the wrist and control the knife, while the other hand delivers a disabling strike to the eyes or throat. The counterattack must be as vicious as possible—anything half-hearted will result in the knife attacker retaliating with the blade.

Some U.S. special forces are trained in the Malaysian knife-fighting martial art of pentjak silat. These specially trained soldiers will even have the confidence to perform a technique that pins the attacker to the floor, the knife still in his or her grasp, but unable to be used. This technique takes real skill, however. Most elite forces soldiers will simply attempt to damage the opponent as severely as possible so that there is little time to use the knife.

Improvised weapons, such as sticks, are also useful, as they can be used to smash the attacker's arm as he or she comes forward with the knife. Police forces around the world are trained to hit a knife-armed attacker's elbows with their batons. The impact causes the attacker to drop the knife, and the arm is rendered useless for further attacks.

PREDICTING VIOLENT ATTACK

In combat, the soldier knows that if he or she encounters the enemy, he or she will have to fight. However, many special forces operations today put soldiers into contact with civilians, which can be tricky—they never know who is going to attack them. This is why a soldier needs to be able to read the signals of impending violence.

The first indicator of an attack is often the person's facial expression and breathing. People about to fight often make large demonstrations that they are about to do so, throwing out their arms to make themselves look physically bigger, shouting to act more aggressive and pump up their courage, and, interestingly, using shorter and shorter sentences as they lead up to the attack (often, they will precede the actual attack with single syllable words, such as "yeah, yeah," repeated quickly). The moment before the actual attack is usually preceded by a sharp intake of breath (to supply oxygen for the effort), and the eyebrows lift up slightly in expectation. The defender will watch for these signals and move quickly out of the range of any possible punch or kick.

The soldier also watches out for a deceptive attack. If a person approaches him or her in a seemingly friendly way, but with darting eyes, pale skin, and a tense mouth—the outward signs of inner aggression—the person may be about to attack. Special care needs to be taken if the person's hands are concealed—he or she may be carrying a knife. In such circumstances, the soldier must order the person to stand at a distance, otherwise defensive actions will be taken.

Today, most soldiers are trained to defuse aggression as it starts. One of the best ways of doing this is simply to keep the aggressive person talking and to make him or her think about his or her actions. Asking questions that require thought-out answers is particularly effective. Saying in a quiet voice, "Explain to me why you are doing this" may get the person talking about his or her feelings, and once he or she does, the actual desire for violence can steadily diminish.

However, the soldier has to be prepared for the situation to flare up at any moment, and may have to use the momentary distraction of the questioning to launch a surprise preemptive attack.

TACKLING A MAN WITH A PISTOL

STEP 1: The soldier held at gunpoint stretches his arms out to the side, hands open, as if in surrender.

STEP 2: With great speed, the soldier spins around, knocking the gun out of the small of his back.

STEP 3: To control the gun, the soldier wraps his left arm around the gun arm and attacks by driving a palm-heel into the enemy's chin.

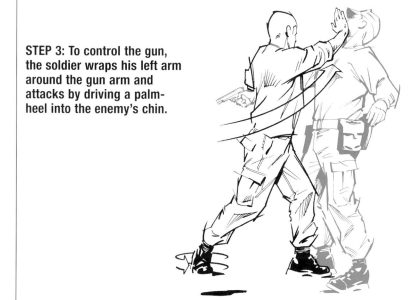

Grappling and Special Techniques

If punches and kicks do not resolve a fight, then the soldier must be prepared to grapple or throw his or her opponent. The aim of grappling is to force the enemy into submission by either imprisoning his or her limbs so that movement is impossible or by applying a chokehold that renders him or her unconscious—or, if the mission demands it, dead.

GRAPPLING

The object of most grapples in military unarmed combat is to apply a chokehold. If this or any other strangulation technique is applied to the enemy's windpipe, cutting off his or her air supply, he or she will be rendered unconscious in about 30 to 60 seconds.

A far more effective technique, however, is to apply pressure on either side of the enemy's windpipe. When the jugular and carotid arteries that run up the side of the neck are compressed hard, blood flow to the brain is stopped. Once this occurs, the enemy will drop down unconscious in as little as five or six seconds, and he or she could be dead within about 30 seconds.

An Israeli soldier applies a restraint. All Israeli men undergo a period of military service in their late teens and early twenties, and instruction in restraint techniques is a priority to help the soldiers cope with civil disturbances, common in Israel.

A DEADLY TECHNIQUE

During World War II, British commandos were trained to dispose of sentries using the headlock choke. They would sneak up behind the sentry, clamp him in this chokehold, and then kick his legs out from under him before walking backwards. The unfortunate sentry would, in effect, be hanged in the commando's arms. Strangleholds are the most lethal grapple, but there are other grapples that do not do as much damage.

The most common chokehold taught to elite forces soldiers is the scissors choke. This technique is performed when the enemy is facing the soldier. In this move, the soldier reaches with his or her right hand and takes hold of the enemy's right collar, gripping the left collar with his or her left hand. The soldier then pulls his or her hands outwards, drawing his or her wrists against the sides of the enemy's throat and strangling. *On no account should you attempt this technique, even for a few seconds, as it may result in irreparable damage to the neck and can be fatal.*

When the enemy has his or her back or side turned to the soldier, a headlock choke is more appropriate. In a right-handed headlock choke, the soldier puts his right arm around the enemy's neck, with the forearm pressing against the throat. The right hand locks into the elbow crease of the left arm, and the left hand goes around the back of the enemy's head. The soldier then locks all parts of the grip together to form a powerful stranglehold.

LOCKING

The lock is a good technique for restraining an enemy whom the soldier does not want to kill. A lock in unarmed combat involves bending or twisting a joint in an unnatural direction, causing great pain and making the joint immobile.

There are three types of joints between the bones in a human skeleton: ball-and-socket, hinge, and movable. A ball-and-socket joint has the end of one bone shaped with a ball-like head, with the ball fitting into a concave socket at the end of the connecting bone. Ball-and-socket joints provide rotational and swinging movements; the shoulder and hip joints are

U.S. soldiers grapple on the floor during training. During the Gulf War, U.S. forces relied constantly on restraint techniques to apprehend and control surrendering Iraqi soldiers, one soldier restraining, while another searched the enemy soldier.

examples of this type of joint. Hinge joints consist of two bones locked together to perform bending and straightening actions on one plane of movement only; the elbows and knees are typical hinge joints. Movable joints are joints in which two bones rock or glide over one another with a limited range of movement; the joints of the spine are one example.

Elite forces soldiers are well aware of how the joints are structured. Many elite units have to complete extensive medical training that involves witnessing autopsies and surgical procedures. During these sessions, they will learn all about the human anatomy and where it is most vulnerable during unarmed combat. Most locks are applied against hinge joints—

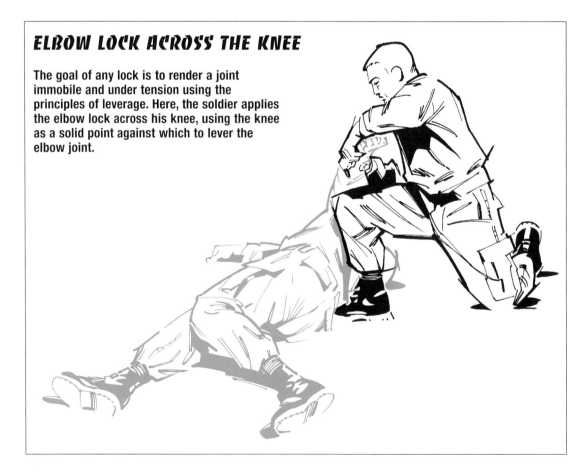

ELBOW LOCK ACROSS THE KNEE

The goal of any lock is to render a joint immobile and under tension using the principles of leverage. Here, the soldier applies the elbow lock across his knee, using the knee as a solid point against which to lever the elbow joint.

DISABLING KNEE LOCKS

The U.S. Army's unarmed combat manual features several knee locks. One of the most painful-looking involves the soldier pushing, in the case of a left-knee lock, his or her left knee hard against the enemy's right knee. By using his or her full body weight, the soldier can force the enemy's knee straight into a lock and then apply even more pressure to break the knee joint. Once the knee is damaged, the enemy will be almost entirely helpless.

typically the elbows and fingers—because it is easy to lock a limb out straight by applying the correct pressure.

A typical arm lock requires that the soldier grab the enemy's right wrist with his or her right hand. The soldier then swings to the left and places his or her left forearm against the back of the enemy's right elbow. By applying hard pressure against the elbow, the joint is locked out straight. The soldier then pushes the enemy to the ground using the lock. Once the enemy is on the ground, he or she is either held there, or the soldier follows up with a finishing technique to disable him or her.

THROWS

Throws are spectacular if performed properly, but they can be downright dangerous for a soldier if they are performed improperly. Throwing is used to put the enemy on the floor, where he or she can be controlled or subjected to a finishing move. If the throw is hard enough, this in itself can

RELEASE FROM A CHOKE

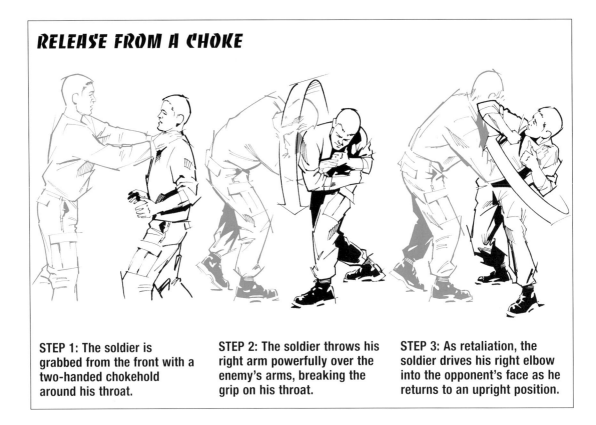

STEP 1: The soldier is grabbed from the front with a two-handed chokehold around his throat.

STEP 2: The soldier throws his right arm powerfully over the enemy's arms, breaking the grip on his throat.

STEP 3: As retaliation, the soldier drives his right elbow into the opponent's face as he returns to an upright position.

injure or knock out the opponent. Throwing a determined enemy takes speed, timing, physical strength, and courage. A throw will work when the soldier uses the enemy's own body weight against him or her, knocking him or her off balance, and then using leverage to throw him or her to the ground.

A soldier must consider a number of factors before deciding to perform a throw. If the enemy is wearing a heavy backpack or chest pouches, a throw may be more difficult. The soldier must also be careful that his or her own pack or straps do not become tangled up in those of his or her enemy, in which case, they may both go crashing to the ground.

The quickest and easiest throw is the sweep. For a right-legged sweep, the soldier places the instep of his or her right foot against the ankle of the enemy's left foot. Next, the soldier sweeps his or her foot hard to the left in a lifting motion and pulls the enemy's left leg from beneath him or her, sending him or her toppling to the ground. To make the throw stronger, the soldier can grab the enemy's collar and pull the enemy's shoulders sharply to the right as he or she sweeps to the left. Sweeps are fast and startling. They

U.S. Army soldiers performing throws and break-falls. Unarmed combat training in the Army usually occurs during Week 3–4 of Basic Training, and it includes fighting with pugil sticks to build aggression.

PERFORMING A BASIC THROW

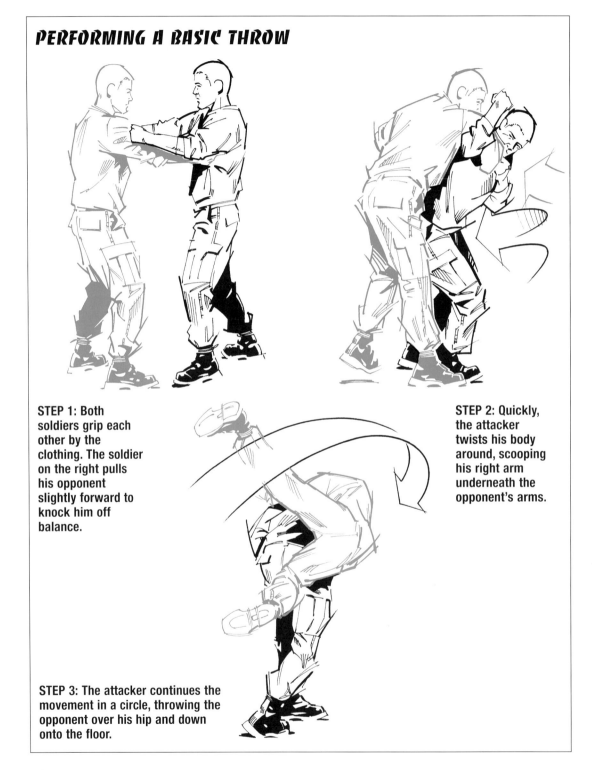

STEP 1: Both soldiers grip each other by the clothing. The soldier on the right pulls his opponent slightly forward to knock him off balance.

STEP 2: Quickly, the attacker twists his body around, scooping his right arm underneath the opponent's arms.

STEP 3: The attacker continues the movement in a circle, throwing the opponent over his hip and down onto the floor.

are also advantageous, in that the soldier does not need to get too close to his or her opponent to perform one.

Throws are often used to escape from strangleholds or grappling attacks. If an enemy approaching from the front grips the soldier in a stranglehold, he or she can execute a hip throw. To do this, the soldier grips the enemy's right sleeve above the elbow with his or her left hand. He or she then twists his or her body 180 degrees so that his or her right hip is placed firmly in the enemy's abdomen and his or her right arm is underneath the enemy's right armpit. Then, in one bold and fast movement, the soldier pulls on the enemy's trapped arm, lifts up and backwards with his or her hip, and pulls the enemy over his or her

ESCAPING FROM A REAR HOLD

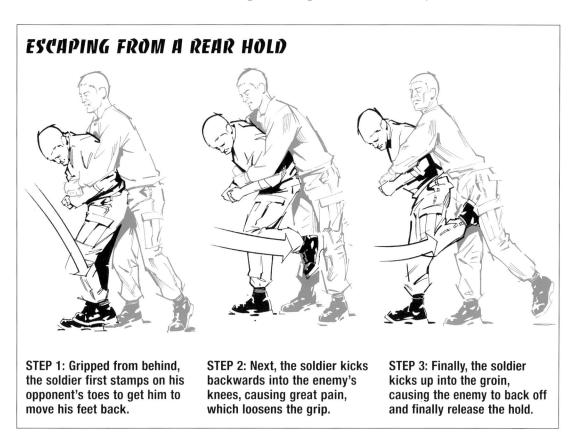

STEP 1: Gripped from behind, the soldier first stamps on his opponent's toes to get him to move his feet back.

STEP 2: Next, the soldier kicks backwards into the enemy's knees, causing great pain, which loosens the grip.

STEP 3: Finally, the soldier kicks up into the groin, causing the enemy to back off and finally release the hold.

shoulder onto the ground. If this move is done properly, the enemy should literally fly through the air and land heavily on his or her back. Once on the ground, the enemy can be finished off.

There are many more throws that can be taught, but special forces soldiers tend to learn only a few movements that are known to work and that can be performed easily. Some U.S. special forces soldiers have had

UNDERARM CHOKE

An underarm choke restricts both blood flow to the brain and breathing, depending on how hard it is applied. Unconsciousness can result in less than five seconds.

SCOOP THROW

STEP 1: The soldier uses a head butt to momentarily stun and distract his opponent and seize the advantage.

STEP 2: Dipping down, he grabs the opponent around both knees as the opponent rocks backwards after the head butt.

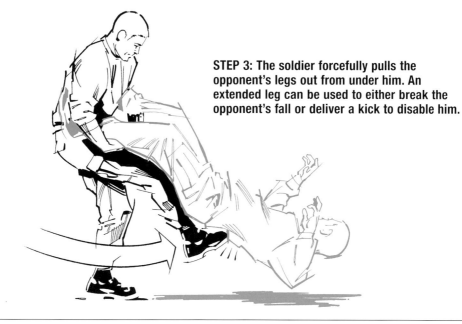

STEP 3: The soldier forcefully pulls the opponent's legs out from under him. An extended leg can be used to either break the opponent's fall or deliver a kick to disable him.

training in aikido (a martial art), which has some of the most complex and difficult throws in the martial arts. However, these are the exception, and sweeps and hip throws tend to be the only techniques instructed.

JUJUTSU

Jujutsu is one of the best martial arts for grappling and throwing techniques. A pure combat skill, it concentrates on defeating an enemy using all available means. It contains many lethal combat techniques, although these are often omitted from modern training. Armies and police forces around the world, however, have relied on its realistic techniques for self-defense purposes. Elements of jujutsu are contained in American, British, and Israeli combat training.

It is uncertain whether jujutsu originated in China or Japan, but an early reference to it was found in a Japanese chronicle from A.D. 712. In this chronicle, there is an account of a man called Tatemi Kazuchi throwing another man like "throwing a leaf." The techniques in jujutsu are believed to have been based on a 13th-century martial art called kumi-tachi, which is described in an ancient book known as the *Konjaku-Monogatari*. Other evidence, however, points to jujutsu originating in China and then being brought to Japan by a monk called Chen Yuanein (1587–1671).

Whatever its origin, jujutsu has long proven itself to be an excellent combat art. Both the samurai and the ninja used its more lethal techniques. Bandits and criminals also found it helped their chosen professions. In fact, the peaceable combat art of judo developed out of jujutsu, when a martial artist named Kano Jiguro (1860–1938) wanted to rid jujutsu of its criminal connotations.

LEG SWEEP

STEP 1: The soldier pushes his opponent to render him off balance and vulnerable to a sweeping attack.

STEP 2: Using his right leg, the soldier hooks his foot around the opponent's left ankle and scoops it off the floor while pulling the soldier over from the shoulders.

STEP 3: Following through, the soldier lifts his opponent's leg high into the air and slams him down onto the floor. Note how the soldier keeps as upright as possible to avoid being dragged down with his opponent.

Glossary

Anti-Semitism	Hostility towards or discrimination against Jews
Bayonet	A steel blade attached at the muzzle end of a rifle or similar gun
Cardiovascular	Relating to the heart and blood vessels
Circuit	A form of physical training that involves performing sequences of exercises at designated locations around a training area
Corps	The main subdivision of an army, usually consisting of two divisions of soldiers
Covertly	Secretly or in disguise
Dojo	A place in which martial arts training is conducted
Fascist	Having a tendency toward strong dictatorial control
Hypothalamus	The part of the brain that regulates body temperature, thirst and hunger
Infiltrate	To gain entrance or access secretly over a period of time
Karate	A Japanese martial art created on the Pacific island of Okinawa in the 16th century. It has become the world's most practiced martial art
Kung fu	An ancient Chinese martial art that consists of many different styles, depending on the teacher and the geographical area of origin; the term means "human effort"
Ninjutsu	Japanese martial art characterized by stealthy movement, espionage, and camouflage

Pancratium	An ancient Greek athletic contest involving both boxing and wrestling
Pikemen	An elite fighting force in Switzerland during the 15th and 16th centuries
Sharpshooter	An expert marksman
Storm troopers	Special assault troops created in Germany during World War I
Superpower	An extremely powerful nation
Surveillance	Close watch kept over someone or something
Telegraph (v.)	To make known by signs, especially unknowingly and in advance

Further Reading

Applegate, Rex. *Kill or Get Killed: Riot Control Techniques, Manhandling, and Close Combat, for Police and the Military.* Boulder, CO: Paladin Press, 1976.

Echanis, Michael D. *Basic Stick Fighting for Combat.* Palm Coast, FL: Black Belt Communications, 1995.

Hayes, Stephen K. *Ninjutsu: The Art of the Invisible Warrior.* New York: McGraw Hill, 1984.

Hollifield, Leonard. *Close-Quarter Combat: A Soldier's Guide to Hand-to-Hand Fighting*. Boulder, CO: Paladin Press, 1997.

Sde-Or, Imi, and Eyal Yanilov. *Krav Maga: How to Defend Yourself Against Armed Assault*. Berkeley, CA: Frog Ltd, 2001.

Sinclaire, Clive. *Samurai: The Weapons and Spirit of the Japanese Warrior*. New York: The Lyons Press, 2001.

U.S. Army Staff Combatives Manual. Boulder, CO: Paladin Press, 2001.

White, Terry. *The SAS Fighting Techniques Handbook*. New York: The Lyons Press, 2001.

Special Forces of the World

Argentina
Falcon Special Operations Brigade (Police)

Australia
Australian SAS (Army)

Belgium

The Paracommando Regiment (Army)

1st Special Reconnaissance Company (Army)

Brazil

Special Forces Detachment (Army)

Marine Special Operations Group (Marines)

Air Force Special Forces (Air Force)

Canada

Special Service Force (Army)

Special Emergency Response Team (Police)

China

6th Special Warfare Group (Army)

8th Special Warfare Group (Army)

Egypt

Special Forces

France

1st Parachute Brigade (Army)

2nd Parachute Brigade (Army)

13th Dragoons Parachute Regiment (Army)

French Foreign Legion Parachute Forces (Army)

Groupe d'Intervention Gendarmerie Nationale (Police)

Germany

Grenzschutzgruppe 9 (Police)

Spezialeinsatzkommados (Police)

India

Parachute Commandos (Army)

Special Frontier Force (Army)

Israel

Mossad (Police/Government)

General Staff Reconnaissance Unit (Army)

Golani Infantry Reconnaissance Unit (Army)

Italy

Paratroop Saboteur Battalion (Army)

Alpini Brigade Mountain Warfare Unit (Army)

Navy Frogmen and Raider's Group (Navy)

Netherlands

104th Long Range Patrol Company (Army)

Royal Netherlands Marine Corps (Marines)

Special Intervention Force (Army)

Russia

Spetsnaz (Army)

Soviet Naval Infantry (Navy)

Special Operations State Militia (Government)

South Africa

Reconnaissance Commandos (Army)

South African Police Special Task Force (Police)

South Korea

707th Special Mission Battalion (Army)

Spain

Spanish Foreign Legion (Army)

Special Operations Group (Police)

United Kingdom

Special Air Service (Army)

Special Boat Service (Marines)

United States

Army Special Forces (Army)

U.S. Navy SEALs (Navy)

U.S. Rangers (Army)

U.S. Marines Recon (Marines)

Delta Force (Army)

Useful Web Sites

U.S. Army Combatives Manual online:

http://www.adtdl.army.mil/

Official Krav Maga web site:

http://kravmaga.com/

Extensive information about martial arts, including schools in your area:

http://www.martialinfo.com/

Assorted links to military martial arts sites:

http://martialarts.about.com/cs/military/

Information about Tukong Moosul, the martial art of Korean Special

Forces: http://tukong.com/

Publisher's Note: The websites listed on this page were active at the time of publication. The publisher is not responsible for websites that have changed their address or discontinued operation since the date of publication. The publisher reviews and updates the websites each time the book is reprinted.

About the Author

Chris McNab is a prolific author and military historian whose books include *Endurance Techniques*, *The SAS Training Manual* and *The SAS First Aid Survival Manual*. His ongoing research projects include the martial arts cultures of the ancient Far East and modern tactics used in low-intensity warfare.

Index

References in italics refer to illustration captions